A SOUL RECHARGED

Book of Affirmations and Journal

VANESSA BARTHEL

authorHOUSE®

AuthorHouse™
1663 Liberty Drive
Bloomington, IN 47403
www.authorhouse.com
Phone: 1 (800) 839-8640

Published by AuthorHouse 06/11/2019

ISBN: 978-1-7283-1531-7 (sc)
ISBN: 978-1-7283-1530-0 (e)

Contents

"NO MUD, NO LOTUS"

-Thich Nhat Hanh

Prelude

I started my day revisiting my first book- A Soul Recharged, A Poetic Journey for the Soul. As I laid there in my bed turning pages of memories, I began to weep! There I was this over forty-year-old woman crying like a newborn baby. It was that one poem, "SOUL MATES" that did me in.

Although the piece has brought joy to many couples. However, some have no idea it was written with both ink and tears! The Truth be told, this poem was written on a cold, lonely, I want to die night!

Unable to function for two weeks,
I remember calling out from work. I stopped all
communication with family, friends, and foes.

Until one night my Soul said enough is enough, now write! I had never taken writing seriously. As a child, I had the plan to do only one thing- sing! I became frustrated at my brain for not wanting to go mute of the pain that I felt. Nevertheless, I was guided to write my thoughts and feeling into a journal instead! It was in my most vulnerable time, that my gift was revived.

I stop crying long enough to pick up a pen and a piece of paper.
For the life of me, I could not understand why my Soul was
saying to me, "this piece will be called SOUL MATES!"

Are you kidding me? Do you see me crying my
heart out because my Lover has left me!
This can not be happening to me. I ask The Universe
for help now my Soul is saying write.

However, I decided to be obedient to what my Soul was saying.
Words started spilling from my heart onto the journal.

I started writing all the things my heart has ever desired! I was able to visualize this Lotus Flower. This Lotus was being rooted from the mug.

Amazingly, for some strange reason, I felt just like that Lotus!
I never imagined that my first journal entry would later become a part of a book!

One of my favorite books is The Secret. One of the quotes made by John
Assaraf states, " Here's the problem. Most people are thinking about what they
don't want and they're wondering why it shows up over and over again!"

What a profound statement by Mr. Assaraf. We sometimes overlook
just how powerful our words truly are! Throughout this book, I
challenge you to write down whatever your heart desires.
Speak life into your situations. Remember, The Universe is always listening!

Dedication

I would like to thank my mother Mable Smith, my children who makes me proud, and Love Ones for your unconditional love and support. To the reader, may you always remember to follow your bliss!

(In memory of Phyllis Armstrong)

A Soul Recharged Daily Affirmations:

I AM Love
I deserve love in return
I manifest great health
I manifest happiness
I manifest peace
I manifest abundance
I embrace new beginnings
I embrace blessings
I embrace good energy
I release anything not growing
I release low vibrations
I release negativity of any kind

THIS JOURNAL BELONGS TO:

"Our prime purpose in this life is to help others. And if you can't help them, at least don't hurt them."

— Dalai Lama

A LIFE INTERRUPTED

I once had a dream
that felt like I had died a thousand lives.

Dreaming of locusts worms eating away at my both my Heart and Soul.
But the nightmare did not stop!

Next, I felt like my eyes had been sealed with the hardest of glues.
I am talking about disappointment glue,
heart-broken glue,
even depression glue.

I still remember that dark day
when all I had left in me was to pray.
Suddenly, as I sat there in shock,
I had this out of body experience.
As I laid there frozen in time,
I watched as my Spirit danced above me
singing "you are being recharged!"

Next to my surprise
I saw my Spirit peeling all of those glues.
It was that very moment that my awakening has begun!

That day, I learned that
only love and light
shall crowd my temple.

-Author Vanessa Barthel

Throughout this book, you will find journal entries that I wrote when my Soul was being recharged. I wanted to share this journey with you. Please know you are not alone.

"ASCENSION"

There are moments
when I feel like this
Carefree Caterpillar
who has became
complacent
To up and downs.
The headaches,
the heartbreaks,
the disappointments,
the people pleasing,
the disrespect,
the turn the other
cheek type etc.
However,
this cocoon
is about to
BURST!
My SOUL
reassured me,
that there's this:
BEAUTIFUL,
INTELLIGENT,
MAGICAL,
POWERFUL,
NO NONSENSE,
BUTTERFLY,
who has been awaiting my ascension.

-Author Vanessa Barthel

"There is no greater agony than bearing an untold story inside you."
-Maya Angelou

"INCOMPLETE"

A dark cloud now fills
the atmosphere.
Nothing left in this space
but some old wasted memories.
It's like that vintage beautiful watch
Yet for years it has lost
Its tick and its tock!
Or
A half painted
house, that love forgot
to complete.
Some try to replace
with superficial items,
Yet nothing can fill
that place called
loneliness.

-Author Vanessa Barthel

Whether you think you can or you think you can't, you're right. – Henry Ford

"SOLITUDE"

There is this place
that I yearn
for.
A
space and time
that haunts
me.
An
unfamiliar wind
that chases
me.
Dreams
of
stillness while
The Hummingbirds serenade
me.
Where
butterflies freely
aviate!
Day in
And Day out,
I
wander
of its
existence.
Perhaps
sitting under this
old rugged tree, helps me find it.

-Author Vanessa Barthel

"The Rugged House"

Empty spaces of time wasted,
a broken window screen that
once housed dreams.
This old house:
innocence lost.
An old screen door
now broken from its hinges;
it once was a door open to many.
An old, rundown fireplace
still burns with memories
of those cold,
bitter winters.
An old couch is still
there. It sits as a
reminder of countless
Lovers who once
played there.
The yard is now overgrown
with thorns, weed and red clay.
Yet I stopped by just
to see the city
demolish it today.
This old house innocent lost.

-Author Vanessa Barthel

"The Love Within"

Clouds and rain,
over and over again
the
same games.
Love
never truly meant
a thing.
Heartbreak was on
every avenue.
Betrayal was there,
as if I didn't
already know it enough.
Blemished images
of
commitment and respect, I was
too naive to be
alone,
yet
too strong to stay.
Countless nights I prayed I'd
hear those two simple words:
"I do!"
Hoping and wishing
that entity would care,
I
almost lost my
Soul
hanging in there.
One
day I had a heartache
so severe
that I thought I would not

even survive.
That day I chose to be the love
that I had been seeking.

-Author Vanessa Barthel

I BELIEVE
IN YOU

Below you will find your own personal journal. Part of becoming recharged is letting go of those things that are hindering us. Be completely honest with yourself. Throughout the journal, you will find exercises to help with your journey.

A SOUL RECHARGED JOURNAL

An Affirmation Day Keeps The Inner Critic Away

Say this affirmation out loud:

"I am glad that I did not give up on myself."

WRITE TWELVE PERSONAL AFFIRMATIONS:

Words are Spells. There's a reason
it's called Spelling! Remember
to use them wisely.

secure
serene glad joyous
close bright tenacious frisky ALIVE OPEN content
merry loving
daring liberated ease fortunate attracted cheerful brave
touched
spirited jubilant reassured kind dynamic animated toward
accepting courageous
comforted affectionate energetic eager determined surprised wonderful calm
delighted encouraged sunny earnest
understanding considerate easy passionate amazed
engrossed
satisfied confident receptive certain unique
sure hopeful
sympathy free and optimistic INTERESTED
lucky overjoyed snoopy
important impulsive great
playful challenged sympathetic concerned keen admiration
nosy enthusiastic provocative loved POSITIVE re-enforced thrilled
intrigued curious inquisitive comfortable
gay devoted STRONG pleased peaceful inspired excited LOVE
hardy affected absorbed interested fascinated drawn
relaxed sensitive HAPPY rebellious anxious tender
blessed thankful gleeful festive elated
bold quiet reliable clever warm
ecstatic GOOD
intent

"I AM"

I AM Spirit.

I AM free.

I AM life.

I AM love.

I AM a Soul Recharged.

I AM awaken.

I AM enlighten.

I AM a believer.

I AM a healer.

I AM a teacher.

I AM a student.

I AM my Brother/Sister keeper.

I AM fearless.

I AM strong.

I AM joy.

I AM peace.

I AM grateful.

I AM open-minded.

I AM compassion.

I AM understanding.

I AM comfort.

I AM perfectly imperfect.

I AM simply me!

-Author Vanessa Barthel

I AND AM ARE TWO IMPORTANT WORDS. THEY CAN ACTUALLY SHIFT OUR ENTIRE LIFE!

I AM

I AM AFFIRMATION NOTES

I have learned over the years that when one's mind is made up, this diminishes fear. –Rosa Parks

Never Give Up

FOLLOW
YOUR BLISS

What if I told you that it's ok to say NO!

MY NO NONSENSE LIST

"THE S ON THE CHEST"

SUPERWOMAN
Walks around with
A big S on her chest.
Saving The Family,
Friends and Foes.
Sending Love and Light
Wherever there's
a leak or a hole!
Flying through LIFE,
trying her best so that

she doesn't have
to use her
Superpowers
twice!
Yet, SUPERWOMAN
has her Kryptonite!
It's has placed her
in situations, where
she forgets the
the word "NO"!
Suddenly,
The S on her chest
stood for stress!
Until one day,
she took off the costume
and placed her crown
upon her head instead!
Remembered the words
"NO" and "SILENCE"

and left those
old people, places
and things
that was dead!

-Author Vanessa Barthel

"THE TEST"

There are times when we have to make hard decisions.
The decisions to love again, trust again,
believe again just to name a few.
What's to do when someone has hurt you?
A feeling so deep that it felt like a cut
into the very core of your Soul!
Well, you are to forgive them.
Yes, you Miss I Cried All Night.
Even you, Mr. They Did Me Wrong.
Besides, your forgiveness is for your growth.
How do we ever expect to be forgiven?
You can remain a prisoner
by wasting time and energy feeling angry and upset.
However, as for me, I choose to forgive and forget.
Remember, life lessons comes with many ups and downs.
Yet the only thing that will always set you free is
The Spirit of Letting Go.

-Author Vanessa Barthel

"You wanna fly, you got to give up the shit that weighs you down."
— Toni Morrison

Letting go can be the hardest yet smartest thing
to do. What do you need to release?

MY LET IT GO AND GROW LIST

According to Webster:
Definition of endurance
1: the ability to withstand hardship or
adversity; especially: the ability to sustain
a prolonged stressful effort or activity.

"RESURGENCE"

I used to search
both High
&
Low.
Seeking Love,
Affection,
Hustle,
Fast Money
&
Flow!
Until one day,
I noticed this
Beautiful Soul
In The Mirror
Staring back
At me!
That day,
I Gave Up
The Ghost.
See
I decided to
Simply LET IT GO!
-Author Vanessa Barthel

"NO MUD, NO LOTUS"
-Thich Nhat Hanh

Too many of us are not living our
dreams because we are living our fears.
–Les Brown

"Fear is the cheapest room in the house. I would like to see you living in better conditions."
-Hafez

"THE COLOR of LOVE"

L-O-V-E
the most misused
word in the world!

Some get it
confused with
lust.

Some
even believe
it not real
unless it hurts!

People spend
a lifetime
searching
for it.

Yet,
too blind
to see it!

This
four letter word
makes some
uncomfortable

solely because
their simple minds
can't
understand how
two Souls
of different race,

Faith
or same sex could
Truly be TwinMates!

The truth
of the matter is,
love is NOT:

black or white,
straight nor gay,
painful, confused,
unsure, money,
sex nor manipulation.

It
Doesn't
Care
If you're
A Christian,
Buddhist,
Muslim
Or
Jew!

Instead
genuine
real love is
a combination
of many
delightful colors!

Love is divine.
Love is commitment.
Love is patience.
Love is peace.
Love is joy.

Love is understanding.
Love should be
You and I.
-Author Vanessa Barthel

A person who never made a mistake
never tried anything new.
— Albert Einstein

NO LIMIT

Gratitude
is
Everything!

"GRATITUDE"

For every lesson
that turned out to be
LIFE blessings,
I AM thankful!

For every great
health report that
I receive,
I AM thankful!

For having the endurance
to follow
my own bliss,
I AM thankful!

For every family, friend
and even foes,
I AM thankful!

For having the courage
to walk my own path,
I AM thankful!

For having the wisdom
to not partake in
anything that means
my Soul no good,
I AM thankful!

For my ink to be
used as a vessel
of love and light,
I AM thankful!

-Author Vanessa Barthel

Below write a list of things that you are grateful for. Remember to visit and add to your list throughout the year.

MY GRATITUDE LETTER

The person who says it cannot be done should not interrupt the person who is doing it. –Chinese Proverbs

You should sit in meditation for 20 minutes a day unless you're too busy. Then you should sit for an hour!

3 KEY MEDITATION BENEFITS:

*1. Helps in balancing our
mind, body, and soul
2. Reduces Stress
3. Increases our feelings of compassion*

MY MEDITATION LOG:

"A couple who OM together, vibrates together."

-Author Vanessa Barthel

"FREEBIRD"

Free to breathe.
Free to love.
Free to be loved.
Free to express myself.
Free to live without stress.
Free to smile.
Free to rest.
Free to forgive.
Free to live.
Free to share.
Free to dare.
Free to dream.
Free to laugh.
Free to bask in happiness.
Free to not partake in anything that causes me sadness.
Free to be completely me.
Free to simply let it be!

-Author Vanessa Barthel

A LETTER TO MY
18-YEAR-OLD SELF:

"Once you know who you are, you don't have to worry anymore."
–Nikki Giovanni

The spiritual path - is simply the journey of living our lives. Everyone is on a spiritual path; most people just don't know it.
-Marianne Williamson

MY PRAYER AND
SCRIPTURE NOTES:

"THE LIGHT"

There
is this light
that burns
so
deep inside
of me.

A
glow
so bright,

that
I must
share in
my
own delight!

The
wisdom
of
knowing
I AM
loved.

An agape
love
that is real
and pure.

See
this light
ignites
with those

who
Spirits
are right

Because
they recognize
me!

Some
have passed
my way
without.

Nevertheless,
I don't mind!

See,
I allow
them to take
of my energy
in hope to ignite
their path.

So
thankful
for my shine.

This light
trust me,

is getting
brighter
time after time.

-Author Vanessa Barthel

"NIRVANA"

Traveling alone
on this road
called
Life,

I stopped
by this old town
called
Yesterday.

In this town,
the streets
were ragged
and
grey.

Therefore,
I decided
not to
stay!

Next
along my path,

I stopped
in a City
called
Compassion.

There
I learned
many lessons.

Yet still
I did not
stay.

Instead,
I drove
East!

I stopped
at a
gas station
called
Forgiveness
and
proceeded
on.

Finally,
after a long dark
bumpy road,

I reached
a Town
called
Nirvana.

There
the streets were
both radiant
and
blissful!

I met
The City's
Mayor
MR. AWAKENING,

who
assured me
that I was
never alone.

For it is there
that my
SOUL
calls home!

-Author Vanessa Barthel

"My mission in life is not merely to survive, but to thrive; and to do so with some passion, some compassion, some humor, and some style."
-Maya Angelou

"Once your purpose
has been revealed, it's like
swimming through
an abyss
to make it to
the shores!"

-Author Vanessa Barthel

No
Matter
What
Comes
Your
Way
Today,

LIVE
Your
TRUTH!
-Author Vanessa Barthel

"A SOUL RECHARGED"

A Soul Recharged
I proudly declare!

My Spirit
bears witness
that hell could
not keep me there.

I am grateful
to still be here.

I once was blind
yet now
I truly see.

Yet some from my past
swear they
know
me.

Old habits
have all disappeared.

Solely because
I have chosen to live!
-Author Vanessa Barthel

"JOY"

No more pain.
No more clouds and rain.
No one to blame.
No more feeling shame.
No more lamentations.
No more limitations.
No more procrastinating.
No more reckless thinking.
No more fears.
No more tears.
I choose to love.
I choose to hug.
I choose to give.
I choose to live.
I choose to simply enjoy!
-Author Vanessa Barthel

On this day,

_____, I

_____completed

**A Soul Recharged Affirmation Journal.
I take an oath to never allow anyone
to steal my joy. Not even myself.**

Printed in the United States
By Bookmasters